CREEPY CREATURES

GHOSTS

Sarah Tieck

Big Buddy Books
An Imprint of Abdo Publishing
abdopublishing.com

abdopublishing.com

Published by Abdo Publishing, a division of ABDO, PO Box 398166, Minneapolis, Minnesota 55439.

Printed in the United States of America, North Mankato, Minnesota.
042015
092015

THIS BOOK CONTAINS RECYCLED MATERIALS

Cover Photo: © Tom Tom/Alamy.
Interior Photos: © AF archive/Alamy (p. 22); Archive Photos/Stringer/Getty Images (p. 25); The Asahi Shimbun/Getty Images (p. 19); ASSOCIATED PRESS (pp. 15, 22, 27); Glow Images (p. 13); ©iStockphoto.com (pp. 7, 11, 15, 23, 29, 30); © Niday Picture Library/Alamy (p. 11); Print Collector/Getty Images (p. 21); © Ronald Grant Archive/Alamy (p. 25); David E. Scherman/Getty Images (p. 17); Shutterstock.com (pp. 5, 9, 13, 24).

Coordinating Series Editor: Rochelle Baltzer
Contributing Editors: Tamara L. Britton, Bridget O'Brien, Marcia Zappa
Graphic Design: Jenny Christensen

Library of Congress Cataloging-in-Publication Data

Tieck, Sarah, 1976-
Ghosts / Sarah Tieck.
pages cm. -- (Creepy creatures)
ISBN 978-1-62403-765-8
1. Ghosts--Juvenile literature. I. Title.
BF1461.T59 2016
133.1--dc23
2015002628

Contents

Creepy Ghosts 4
Scary Stories 6
Types of Ghosts 10
Haunted History 12
Around the World 16
What Do They Want? 20
Ghosts in Pop Culture 22
Fact or Fiction? 26
What Do You Think? 28
Let's Talk 30
Glossary 31
Websites 31
Index 32

Creepy Ghosts

For centuries, people have told spooky stories about ghosts. They describe groaning voices and ghostly screams. People hear footsteps, then look and no one is there.

Ghosts have appeared in books, stories, plays, television shows, and movies. But are they real, or the stuff of **legend**? Let's find out more about ghosts, and you can decide for yourself!

Some people have reported seeing ghostly figures looking out of windows.

Scary Stories

A ghost is the spirit of a person who has died. People often think of ghosts as **transparent** or invisible. Ghosts can pass through walls and doors.

How do you know if a ghost is present? You might notice a cold spot in a room. You might hear voices or crying or smell strange odors. Objects may move or doors may slam, seemingly on their own.

Did you know?

Some ghosts are evil beings.

Ghosts may appear solid or see-through.

Ghosts are found in many places. Some ghosts haunt houses or other buildings. Others haunt outdoor areas, such as battlefields. And, some hang out in graveyards. Ghosts that have unfinished business may be found close to where they died.

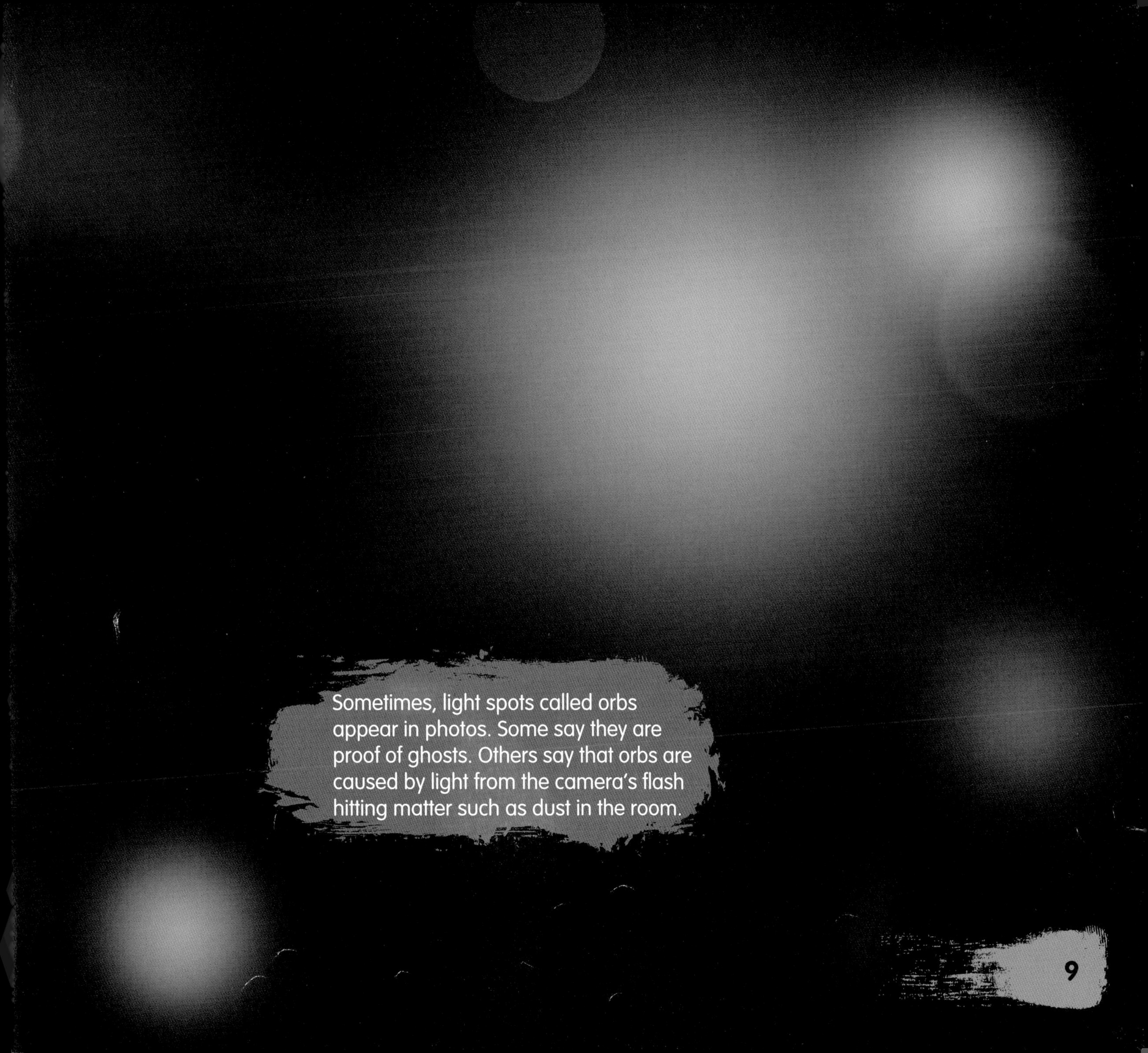

Sometimes, light spots called orbs appear in photos. Some say they are proof of ghosts. Others say that orbs are caused by light from the camera's flash hitting matter such as dust in the room.

Types of Ghosts

There are different types of ghosts. People and animals can appear as ghosts. Even objects, such as planes or ships, can be ghosts.

Noisy spirits called poltergeists (POHL-tuhr-gistes) are considered harmful. They are invisible, but scary. They may throw things, slam doors, turn lights on and off, and pound on walls.

Did you know?

Experts say poltergeists may not be ghosts. Instead, they may be supernatural forces, which cannot be explained by science.

Some people believe dogs or other animals can sense ghosts in a room.

Some say the ghost of President Abraham Lincoln's funeral train appears every year around the time of his death.

Haunted History

Ghost stories go back hundreds of years. Presidents, first ladies, and workers claim to have seen ghosts in the White House in Washington DC. Many say they have seen the ghosts of former presidents, such as Abraham Lincoln.

Another haunted place is Saint Louis Cemetery No. 1. It is in New Orleans, Louisiana. This graveyard contains more than 100,000 bodies. Some of the spirits of the dead are said to haunt the cemetery.

People say the ghost of voodoo queen Marie Laveau walks among the graves in Saint Louis Cemetery No. 1. She died in 1881.

First Lady Eleanor Roosevelt said she felt the presence of Abraham Lincoln's ghost in the White House.

A famously haunted house is in Amityville, New York. In 1974, a murder happened in the home. Soon after, another family moved in. They said the house was haunted. Ghost hunters also claimed the home was filled with evil spirits.

Alcatraz prison near San Francisco, California, is also said to be haunted. It once held some of the country's most dangerous criminals. Al Capone is one famous prisoner who spent time there. Some say they've heard the sound of his banjo playing.

The story of the Amityville house has been retold in books and movies.

Alcatraz is located on an island in San Francisco Bay. The waters surrounding it made escape nearly impossible.

Around the World

Ghost stories are part of **cultures** around the world. In Europe, people believed spirits could return to the world on Samhain (SOWUH-n). On November 1, long-ago **Celts** would honor the start of winter with this feast day.

There are many old, haunted places in Europe. Some people believe one of the most haunted homes was Borley Rectory in Essex, England. Borley Rectory was built in 1863. It burned down in 1939.

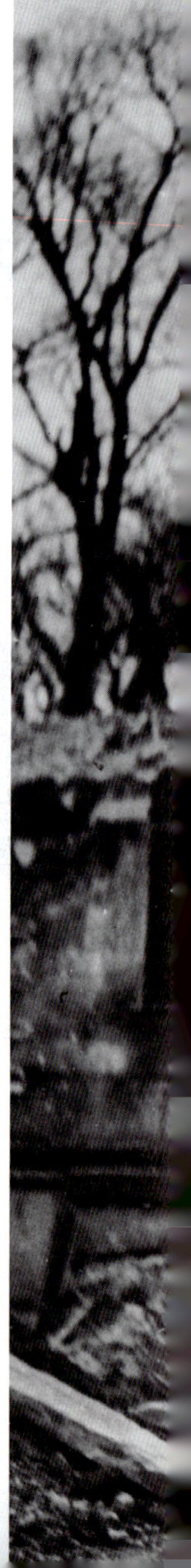

Did you know?

A man named Harry Price studied the Borley Rectory hauntings. Some say Price is the father of modern ghost hunting.

The ghosts at Borley Rectory threw objects at people, wrote on the walls, and rang bells.

In Spanish-speaking parts of North and South America, people tell folk stories about ghosts. These include the crying ghost called La Llorona. She is trapped on earth looking for her children.

In Japan, many honor the dead in late summer. They do this to protect their families from ghosts who may want to harm them. They visit graves and clean them. They also prepare special meals and chant.

Did you know?

In Japan, the word for "ghost" is *yurei* (yoo-ray-ee). There are different types of yurei. But most have long, black, messy hair. And, they wear white clothing.

The Japanese call and send away spirits in the middle of July or August. This time is called *Bon*.

What Do They Want?

Many stories tell of ghosts reaching out to the living. Some ghosts simply appear. Others try to help a person or give someone a message.

In the 1800s, **mediums** held **séances** to **communicate** with ghosts, or spirits. Today, some people still do this. There are also **ceremonies** and **rituals** to get rid of ghosts. And, some people try to help spirits give messages or cross to the next world.

Did you know?

Some believe that mediums are playing tricks on others.

In the 1800s, many people belonged to a movement called Spiritualism. They often gathered to contact spirits.

Casper the Friendly Ghost

Casper was created around 1940. This friendly ghost became the star of many cartoons. In 1995, the movie *Casper* came out.

Hogwarts Ghosts

In J.K. Rowling's Harry Potter books, Hogwarts School of Witchcraft and Wizardry has many ghosts. Peeves is a mischievous poltergeist. Nearly Headless Nick is helpful. Moaning Myrtle haunts a bathroom.

Ghosts in Pop Culture

A Christmas Carol

In 1843, Charles Dickens printed *A Christmas Carol.* In this book, ghosts visit Ebenezer Scrooge. His dead friend Jacob Marley returns as a ghost to help him. Then, Scrooge meets three spirits. They show him his past, present, and future. They change his life.

Scooby-Doo

Scooby-Doo has been in movies and television shows since 1969. This funny dog and his friends solve mysteries. Sometimes, the characters come upon ghosts. Usually, the ghosts are proven to be fake.

Ghostbusters

Ghostbusters is a funny movie from 1984. In it, a group of male ghostbusters fight spirits in New York City, New York. In 2015, this movie was being remade with a group of female ghostbusters.

Poltergeist

Poltergeist is a famous scary movie from 1982. In it, a family has to fight evil spirits in their home to save the youngest daughter.

Fact or Fiction?

People have different ways of thinking about ghosts. Some think of ghosts as spirits to remember and honor. Others feel afraid of them. Still others don't believe in ghosts at all.

Some people use special tools to try to prove ghosts really exist. Ghost hunters visit haunted places. They search for **evidence** of ghostly activity or another type of haunting.

Ghost hunters take photos, record sounds, and gather other scientific information.

What Do You Think?

Do ghosts still send a chill up your spine? It can be fun to tell spooky ghost stories or visit haunted houses.

It is also interesting to learn about the history behind famous ghost stories. Knowing what is true and what is made up is powerful. Whether you read a ghost story or go on a ghost hunt, you are in for an interesting journey.

Dressing like a ghost is popular on Halloween. All you need is a white sheet and some scissors to make a costume!

Let's Talk

What ghost stories do you know?

What would you do if you encountered a ghost?

How would it feel to be part of a ghost hunt?

If you were to write a ghost story, what would be your ghost's reason for haunting?

How are the ghosts in movies and books different from the ghosts people say they have seen in real life? How are they the same?

Glossary

Celts (KEHLTS) people who lived about 2,000 years ago in many countries of western Europe.

ceremony a formal event on a special occasion.

communicate (kuh-MYOO-nuh-kayt) to give and receive information, such as knowledge or news.

culture (KUHL-chuhr) the arts, beliefs, and ways of life of a group of people.

evidence facts that prove something is true.

legend an old story that many believe, but cannot be proven true.

medium a person who can talk to the spirit world.

ritual (RIH-chuh-wuhl) a formal act or set of acts that is repeated.

séance (SAY-ance) a meeting at which people attempt to make contact with the dead.

transparent able to be seen through.

Websites

To learn more about Creepy Creatures, visit **booklinks.abdopublishing.com**. These links are routinely monitored and updated to provide the most current information available.

Index

Abraham Lincoln's funeral train **11**

Alcatraz prison **14, 15**

Amityville house **14, 15**

appearance **6, 7, 10, 18**

Borley Rectory **16, 17**

California **14**

Casper **22**

Christmas Carol, A **23**

England **16**

Europe **16**

ghost hunting **14, 17, 25, 26, 27, 28**

Ghostbusters **25**

Harry Potter books **22**

Japan **18, 19**

Louisiana **12**

New York **14, 25**

North America **18**

Poltergeist **25**

poltergeists **10, 22**

Saint Louis Cemetery No. 1 **12, 13**

Scooby-Doo stories **24**

South America **18**

Spiritualism **21**

White House **12, 13**